Good Hugs
and
Bad Hugs

How Can You Tell?

by Angela R. Carl

illustrated by Richard D. Wahl

STANDARD PUBLISHING
Cincinnati, Ohio   2962

How to Use This Book

To the parent/teacher:

This activity book is intended for use with the parent/teacher book, *Child Abuse! What You Can Do About It,* to train children in sexual abuse prevention. Acquaint yourself with the adult book information and total program before you begin teaching. The adult book provides lesson objectives and easy-to-follow teaching suggestions as well as supplemental activities to accompany the lessons in this book.

The course may be taught by parents at home or by a teacher to a small group of children who are close in age. Lesson discussions and activities may be adapted to a child's age and level of understanding from grades K-6.

The primary goal of this program is to help prevent the student from becoming a victim of child sexual abuse. The program is designed to teach children about the danger of sexual abuse in a nonthreatening way, how to identify potentially dangerous situations, how to avoid abuse, how to deal with it if it happens, and how to seek help from a trusted adult. Additional benefits of the instruction include:

● the building of a child's self-esteem,

● an increased confidence and ability to stand up for his rights in situations of personal injustice other than sexual abuse,

● the development of positive patterns for making decisions that will apply in later years to other problems such as alcohol/drug abuse and premarital sex,

● knowledge about how to use support systems to help with any problem,

● enhancement of the parent/child relationship through the sharing of personal feelings and intimate conversations.

Set aside a place and time when you can work together uninterrupted. Limit sessions to twenty to forty-five minutes, depending upon the child's age and attention span.

Approach the course as a continuation of safety instruction, reminding your child of the importance of fire safety, water safety, traffic safety, home safety, and so on. Tell him that this course is another important kind of safety—personal body safety.

Observe your child's reactions as you teach to see if he needs more information or reinforcement. If your child seems overly uncomfortable, gently explore why. His discomfort could be an indication that he has been abused. Patiently clarify misconceptions and review main points repeatedly.

If you are teaching a class, meet with the parents first to explain the program. Stress that it will be nonthreatening personal safety instruction, not sex education.

Begin by setting a serious tone and laying some ground rules. At the first sign of silliness, acknowledge that sexual abuse is uncomfortable to talk about, so people sometimes show their embarrassment by giggling. Assure the children that you do not intend to embarrass them personally, and you will not allow anyone in the class to embarrass another class member. Provide a question box so children may ask questions anonymously if desired.

If a child begins to disclose abuse during a class, tell him you will speak with him privately. Chapter 6 of the adult book tells how to respond to disclosures of abuse.

One of the most important teaching techniques for personal body safety is the presentation and discussion of "what-if" situations. These situations should stimulate the child's thinking and decision-making skills. If he proposes unrealistic solutions, help him discover why they wouldn't work. Guide him to more realistic solutions.

Begin each lesson with a review. After the course has been completed, provide reinforcement of the concepts from time to time. Knowledge about personal body safety should be expanded as children grow older.

Scripture:
"From the Holy Bible, New International Version. Copyright © 1973, 1978, 1984 International Bible Society. Used by permission of Zondervan Bible Publishers."

ISBN 0-87403-007-2

Copyright © 1985 by Angela R. Carl.
Published by The STANDARD PUBLISHING Company, Cincinnati, Ohio.
Division of STANDEX INTERNATIONAL Corporation.
Printed in U.S.A.

I AM SPECIAL TO GOD!

Jesus called the   *to him and said, "Let the little*
come to me, and do not hinder them, for the
of   *belongs to such as these."*   **—Luke 18:16**

God loves _____ .
(your name)

He gave me a MIND and a BODY that is not like anyone else's. He wants me to use my MIND and my BODY to honor Him.

I praise you because I am fearfully and   *made; your*
are wonderful. I know that full well.   **—Psalm 139:14**

I am custom-made by God.

PRESENTING ...   (NAME)

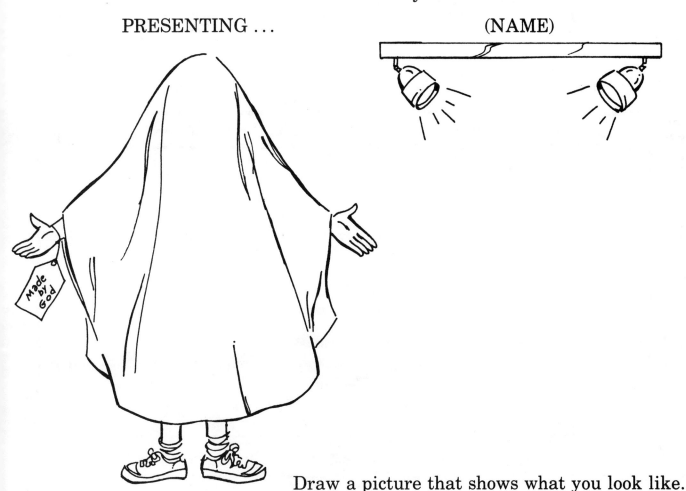

Draw a picture that shows what you look like.

I CAN DO MANY THINGS

Make a list or draw pictures of the things
you are good at or just like to do.

GOD WANTS ME TO BE SAFE

I need to use my MIND to keep my BODY safe from harm.

What could your MIND tell you to do to help keep your BODY safe in each picture below?

GOD GAVE ME SENSES TO HELP ME KNOW WHAT IS GOING ON AROUND ME

Blessed are your   because they   , and your   because they
.   **—Matthew 13:16**

*   and see that the Lord is good.*   **—Psalm 34:8**

If the whole body were an ear, where would the sense of   be? **—1 Corinthians 12:17**

People were bringing little   to   to have him   them.
                                                                              —Mark 10:13

My SENSES send messages to my MIND.

My SENSES help me decide whether or not I like something.

My SENSES can help keep me safe. They are my built-in radar system.

1. Draw a line and match each SENSE with the correct body part.
2. Draw a line and match each SENSE with the picture that shows how it can help you keep safe.
3. Circle the one SENSE that uses your whole body.

MY SENSE OF TOUCH
IS VERY IMPORTANT

Draw the correct body part to fill in the boxes.

I can only see with my ☐, hear with my ☐, smell with my ☐,

and taste with my ☐, but I can feel TOUCHES with ALL my body parts.

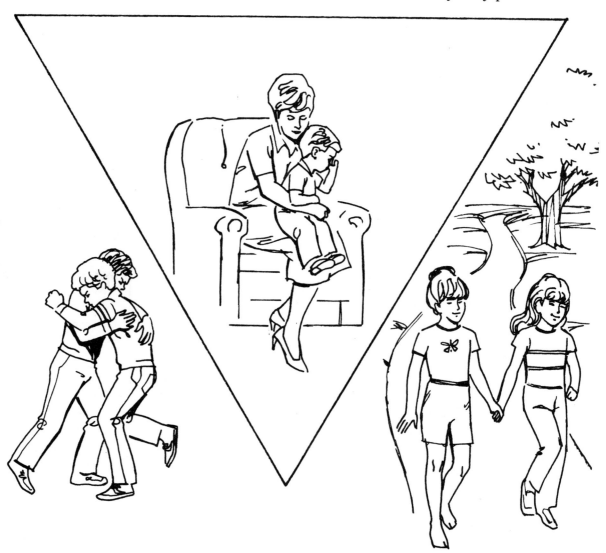

People touch other people in many different ways.

1. Draw a heart on the people who are touching someone in a way that makes him/her happy.

2. Draw an X on the people who are touching someone in a bad way.

3. Talk with your parents or teacher about what is happening in each picture.

GOD WANTS PEOPLE TO TOUCH EACH OTHER IN GOOD WAYS

He (Jesus) took the children in his   *, put his*   *on them and blessed them.*
—Mark 10:16

Snuggles, hugs, and kisses from those we love make us feel happy.

While you color this picture, name all the good touches you can think of.

GOOD TOUCHES
MAKE ME FEEL GOOD

Draw a picture that shows

when someone touched you in a good way.

How did you feel when the person touched you this way?

_____

_____

SOME TOUCHES
DO NOT FEEL GOOD

Sometimes people do not touch others in the ways that God wants them to. They do not follow the Golden Rule:

"In everything, do to   what you would have them do to   ."—**Matthew 7:12**

Draw a picture that shows when someone touched you in a way that you did not like.

Describe how you felt when the person touched you in this way.

_____

_____

_____

SOMETIMES HUGS OR OTHER GOOD TOUCHES CAN BE CONFUSING

Good touches can sometimes feel bad or confusing when:

- We are not expecting them.
- The touch is from a stranger or someone we don't know well.
- The touch becomes uncomfortable.
- We feel embarrassed by the touch.

How do you think the children in these pictures felt about these touches?

MY BODY BELONGS TO ME

Read 1 Corinthians 6:20.
I can use my MIND to try to stop touches I do not like.

Look back at the pictures on page 13. The children in these pictures did not like the touches they were receiving.

Sharon had a problem like this, too. Every time Uncle Frank came to visit, he would pick her up and squeeze her tightly. Sometimes he kissed her on the lips and asked her to give him a kiss. Sharon liked Uncle Frank, but she hated the way he hugged and kissed her. She wished he would stop. Sharon knew that God wanted her to feel happy when someone touched her. But Uncle Frank's hugs and kisses made her feel bad.

One day she decided to do something about it. As soon as he picked her up, she said, "Uncle Frank, I'm happy to see you, but would you please put me down? I do not like to be squeezed so hard." It was a difficult thing to say, but Sharon was glad she had said it.

Uncle Frank was surprised. He put her down and apologized. "Sharon, I only hugged and kissed you because I like you so much. But if you really don't want me to do that, I won't. How about if we just shake hands?"

Sharon smiled. "Thank you, Uncle Frank, for understanding how I feel."

If someone touches me in a way I don't like, I have the right to say,

_____

_____

_____

SOME PARTS OF MY BODY ARE PRIVATE

The _____ is a unit, though it is made up of many _____ ; and though all its _____ are many, they form one _____
—1 Corinthians 12:12

Can you name all the parts of your body?

The *private parts* of my body are the parts that are covered by a swimsuit or my underwear.

PRIVATE MEANS "HANDS OFF"

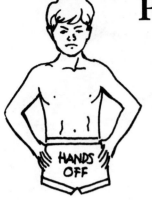

Most of the time it is NOT OK for anyone, even someone I love, to touch my private parts.

Can you think of a time when it would be OK for an adult to touch your private parts?

_____

_____

_____

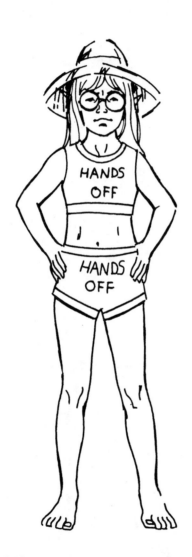 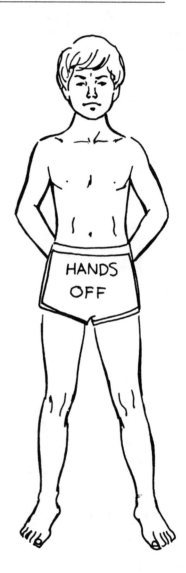

It is NEVER OK for an adult to touch a child's private parts if he or she asks the child to keep it a secret.

It is NEVER OK for an adult to ask a child to touch his or her private parts.

In fact, this kind of touching is against the law. It is called _sexual abuse_.

16

SOMETIMES I NEED TO SAY "NO!"

Saying "No!" to someone older than you are can be very hard, especially if the person is someone you like.

Pretend someone said to you, "Take off your clothes so I can teach you about the differences between boys and girls."
Of course you should say "No!" But how do you say it?
Place a check mark above the best way to say "No!" pictured below.

Practice saying "No!" in a confident way when your teacher or parent reads each sentence below.

- Your classmate whispers during a test, "Move your hand so I can copy your answers."
- An older and bigger student corners you in the rest room at school. "Give me your lunch money!" he(she) demands.
- While shopping with your aunt she says, "Put that cassette tape in your pocket. The salesclerk isn't watching."
- At camp while you are getting ready for bed, the counselor comes and sits on your bed. He has a dirty magazine. "Look at these pictures. You'll like them," he says.

17

SAY "NO!" — THEN GO!

If your senses tell you that something is wrong about the way in which a person talks to you or touches you, say "No!" Then get away. While you color the picture below, talk with your parent or teacher about ways you can get away.

SOME SECRETS MUST BE TOLD

Can you think of some secrets that are "good secrets" because they are kept to surprise someone in a happy way?
Can you think of some bad secrets?

One kind of secret that is very bad is when someone touches your private parts or asks you to touch theirs. The person who abused you may tell you to keep it a secret. The person may even try to scare you so you won't tell anyone.

He/she may say, "This is our special game. Don't tell anyone else about it."
He/she could say, "I'll give you a bicycle *(or something else you want)* if you don't tell about this."
Or he/she might say, "Something terrible will happen to you if you tell about this. Your mother or father will send you away."
He/she might even say, "I will kill you if you tell anyone."

If this happens to you, you will need to do something about it, or it might happen again. You must tell an adult you trust about the secret so he or she can help you.

WHO COULD YOU TELL?

"God is our refuge and strength, an ever present
in   ."   **—Psalm 46:1**

Everybody needs to ask for help sometimes. It is important to know who you can turn to when you have a problem. We can always talk to God when we need help. But sometimes we need to ask for help from adults, too.

Write your name on the umbrella handle below. Write "God" inside the point at the top. Then write in the sections of the umbrella the names of the people you could ask for help. Include family members, teachers, neighbors, ministers, and other adults you trust.

What would you do if the first person you told did not believe you or try to help you?_____

WHERE DO I BELONG?

Draw faces of yourself and the adults you live with in the circles. Can you fill in all the blanks? If not, ask your parent or teacher for help.

1. My name is _____ .
2. My father's name is _____ .
3. My mother's name is _____ .
4. If you live with someone other than your father or mother, what is his/her name? _____ .
5. Draw a picture of the house or building you live in.
6. My house or apartment number is _____ .
7. The name of the street I live on is _____ .
8. The name of the town or city I live in is _____ .
9. The name of my state is _____ .
10. My zip code is _____ .
11. My telephone number is (__ __ __) __ __ __ - __ __ __ __ .
12. My parent(s) work at _____ .
13. Emergency telephone number besides my own number (__ __ __)

   __ __ __ - __ __ __ __ .

Sing "Jesus Loves Me" with your parent or teacher. Then substitute the correct words in the song to tell important information about yourself. Follow the example below.

Jesus loves Anya Carl,
She lives at 161 Arnold Drive,
In the town of Kingston,
In the state of New York.

Yes, Jesus loves her,
Yes, Jesus loves her,
Yes, Jesus loves her,
The Bible tells her so.

Jesus loves Anya Carl,
She knows how to call her home.
She dials area code 914-
339-1602.

Yes, Jesus loves her,
Yes, Jesus loves her,
Yes, Jesus loves her,
The Bible tells her so.

LEARN HOW TO USE A VERY IMPORTANT HELPER

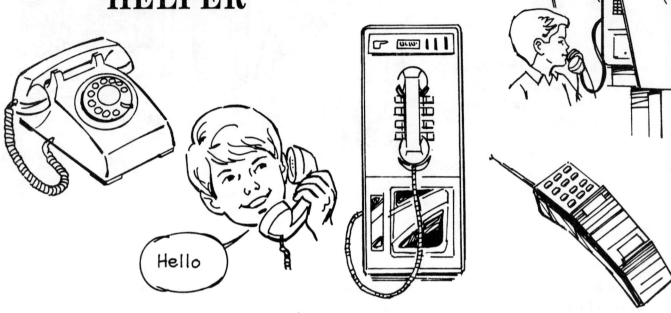

Do you know how to use the different kinds of telephones? Ask your parents or teacher to show you how to use a pay phone.

What should I say if someone I don't know
calls when I'm home alone?

_____

_____

Talk it over. Your parents or teacher can help you learn what to say.

Who can I call if I need help?
NAME   PHONE NUMBER

1. _____   _____
   (parent at work)
2. _____   _____
   (relative or friend)
3. _____   _____
   (neighbor)
4. Fire department   _____
5. Police department   _____
6. Hospital   _____

Print important phone numbers on a small card and place it on or near your phone.

DO YOU REMEMBER WHAT YOU HAVE LEARNED?

Test your memory about what you have studied so far in this book. Try to fill in the blanks of the sentences below with the correct words. Then print them in the crossword puzzle. The clues are numbered with arrows pointing down or across for the puzzle. If you have trouble, look at the word list on page 31.

1__ __ __ made me, and He wants me to use my 2__ __ __ __ and my 3__ __ __ __ to honor Him.

I can use my 4__ __ __ __ __ __ to help keep my body safe. I can 5__ __ __ __ the sense of 6__ __ __ __ __ with all my body parts.

Most people touch others in 7__ __ __ __ ways, but sometimes people touch others in ways that feel 8__ __ __ . 9__ __ __ __ usually feel good, but sometimes they can feel bad.

I can say 10"__ __ !" if someone tries to touch the 11__ __ __ __ __ __ __ parts of my body or asks me to touch his or her 11__ __ __ __ __ __ __ parts.

If my senses tell me that something could be wrong, I should try to 12__ __ __ __ __ __ __ *(two words)*.

If an adult tells me to keep a 13__ __ __ __ __ __ about touching, I should 14__ __ __ __ another adult that I trust.

If no one is around to help me when I have a problem, I can use a 15__ __ __ __ __ __ __ __ __ to call for help.

FREDDY'S PROBLEM

Most adults like children and do not want to harm them. But there are some people in the world who try to touch children in bad ways. Touching the private parts of a child's body is called *sexual abuse*. Read about one boy who had a problem with *sexual abuse*.

Freddy was a star player for the best Little League baseball team in town. Freddy could hit the ball farther, throw it harder, and run faster than anyone else on the team. Coach Charlie was excited to have such a good player on his team. Sometimes Coach Charlie picked up Freddy after school and took him to practice at a nearby park. Coach Charlie and Freddy's father were good friends, so Freddy's parents never worried about Freddy while he was with Coach Charlie.

One day after practice, Coach Charlie put his hand on Freddy's shoulder as he always did when they walked toward the car. "You are some ballplayer, Freddy. I'm going to buy you a special glove that will help you to play even better," he said.

"Wow!" exclaimed Freddy. He had wanted a new glove for a long time. This was too good to be true. "That's terrific, Coach. Do you really mean it?" he asked excitedly.

"Of course," smiled his coach as they got into the car. "We'll go over to the sporting goods store in a few minutes. But, first, I want to show you another way to have fun besides playing baseball. You are very special to me, Freddy. I like you a lot."

Then Coach Charlie gently put his hand inside Freddy's pants and touched his private parts.

Freddy just stared in surprise at Coach Charlie. He did not like this kind of touching, but he had always trusted Coach Charlie. He didn't want to hurt his feelings. Besides, Coach Charlie was going to buy him a new glove. But this kind of touching made him feel *yukky* inside. Freddy felt confused!

Pretend you are a fly who could buzz in Freddy's ear at this moment and tell him what to do. What three important things should Freddy do?

1. _____
2. _____
3. _____

Discuss with your parent or teacher:

- How was the way Coach Charlie touched Freddy in the car different from when he put his hand on his shoulder?
- Why did Freddy feel confused?
- What would you do if you were Freddy?
- What would you say to Freddy's parents if you were he?
- What do you think Freddy's parents will say after he tells them?
- What could Freddy do if his parents don't believe him?
- Was the problem Freddy's fault?

USE YOUR MIND TO HELP KEEP YOU SAFE

What would you do if you became separated from your parents at a busy shopping mall? Think about it while you color the picture below. Then write your answer on the lines below.

WHO IS A STRANGER?

A *stranger* is a person that you and your family do not know. Even if someone you do not know talks to you in a friendly way, he or she is still a stranger. People you see every day are strangers if you and your family have never talked with them.

Some people think that strangers look like this person.

Mark an S over the head of each person in the picture below who could be a stranger.

TRUST YOUR BUILT-IN RADAR, YOUR SENSES, TO HELP YOU KNOW WHEN SOMETHING MIGHT BE WRONG

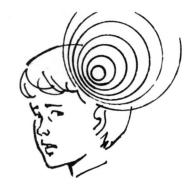

Most strangers do not want to harm children, but some do. Because of these few bad strangers, it's important to be careful around all strangers.

Something might be wrong when:

- a stranger asks you for information.
- a stranger wants to take your picture.
- a stranger asks you to help him/her find a lost pet.
- two friendly strangers drive up in a car and tell you your parents have asked them to bring you home.

WHAT WOULD YOU DO IF ...

.... a stranger in a park, or someone you know very well, showed his/her private parts to you?

WHAT WOULD YOU DO IF . . .

. . . . your baby-sitter showed you a magazine with pictures of people with no clothes on, hugged you, or promised you a nice surprise if you would take off your clothes?

WHAT WOULD YOU DO IF ...

.... you were visiting a neighbor you knew well and he hugged you, then promised to give you money if you let him touch your private parts?

Word list for the puzzle on page 25: Touch. Private. Mind. Get away. Secret. Feel. Telephone. God. Senses. Tell. Body. Good. Hugs. Bad. No.

GOD LOVES YOU
AND WANTS YOU TO BE SAFE
NO MATTER WHAT

"How great is the   *the Father has lavished on us, that we should be called*

of   *! And that is what we are!"*   *—1 John 3:1*